DAVID MUENCH'S

Cherish The Land, Walk In Beauty

ARIZONA

CONTENTS

FOREWORD

8

INTRODUCTION

David Muench was born to

photography like a Kennedy

to politics.

15

LIGHT

Light gives meaning to form. …

For me, light is the ultimate

affirmation of life.

20

4

FORM

When you photograph a

dune, you capture forever a

form that will exist for only

a moment. For me, that's a

very powerful act.

52

LIFE

I often wonder: with all our

technology, have we really

learned anything about

Nature except how to

suppress it?

86

ECOLOGY

I search for harmony in things.

I try to bring opposites together.

That's a lot of what my

photography is about.

118

FOREWORD

TEXT BY STEWART L. UDALL

David Muench's search for landscapes that widen our appreciation of the mysteries and messages of the natural world has taken him on wide-ranging photo expeditions to North America's mountains, plains, and valleys. Images he captured on film have appeared in more than 30 large-format books, and lovers of our region's varied enclaves of beauty should savor his statement that he considers Arizona his "spiritual home."

To fully appreciate the work of any artist, one should acquire insights into the beliefs that animate that person's vision. For this reason, I urge those who pick up this book to begin, not by flipping through the pages of stunning photographs, but rather by reading David's essays at the start of each chapter to explain his lifelong infatuation with Arizona's diverse array of striking landscapes.

The photographs in this book range from expansive scenic vistas to intimate shots of desert environments, from the textures of slick rock in hidden slot canyons to images framed by the "sky islands" of the Sonoran Desert. To David Muench, "Arizona is a miraculous place …

TODAY ARIZONA HAS MORE LEGALLY DESIGNATED WILDERNESS AREAS THAN ANY OTHER STATE.

because it is a land of such extremes, such strangeness." To him, "The Sonoran Desert is the most lush, most varied, most dramatic desert on Earth." Moreover, by not overemphasizing the Grand Canyon or the soaring monoliths in Monument Valley, he reminds us that "powerful form exists everywhere in Arizona, not just in mountains and canyons."

For me, a fascinating part of David's essays relate to artistic insights he shares about how "magic lives in the light" and how certain kinds of reflected light transform "the whole character of the landscape." When he declares that "light is the ultimate affirmation of life," David reveals one of the keys to his artistic skills as a photographer.

He also explains that what he calls the "quiet hours" — "just before dawn, just after sunset, deep in fog … or in the wake of a summer thunderstorm when the air has an unearthly stillness and the light isn't sure what it is to become" — often provide a delicate backdrop for memorable images. David makes us understand that those who rise early — or who study the exquisite strands of light after the sun has set — see beauty the rest of us miss.

It is logical that many of the best photographs in this book were taken in wild, open spaces protected as untrammeled areas under provisions of the Wilderness Act of 1964. David expresses his passion for wild country with these words:

"We need places where there is no trace of human interference, because these places will then serve as a standard. We need these places because they cleanse us."

One of the reasons Arizona grips David's imagination is that our state has set the pace in wilderness protection in the West. Today Arizona has more legally designated wilderness areas (92) than any other state. It also has the largest number of BLM land units (47) under the umbrella of the Wilderness Act.

This came about because in the 1970s and '80s Arizona had two leaders in Congress — Senator Barry Goldwater and Representative Morris K. Udall — who wanted to permanently preserve Arizona landscapes they loved. The upshot was that Barry and Mo collaborated to pass a series of wilderness bills that gave our state a splendid legacy of pristine places. Future generations who enjoy Arizona's secluded cathedrals will owe homage to the pioneering work of these farsighted native sons.

Shortly after being elected to a fourth term as an Arizona congressman, Stewart L. Udall was appointed by President John F. Kennedy to serve as Secretary of the Interior. Among his responsibilities during eight years as secretary was the administration of the Wilderness Act of 1964. He initiated programs that helped bring the ecological revolution to fruition.

An avid reader, Udall arranged for Robert Frost to read poetry at President Kennedy's inauguration. Later Frost accompanied Udall on a trip to the Soviet Union.

Udall's first book, a best-seller entitled *The Quiet Crisis* (1963), advanced the proposition that people must grasp the relationship between human stewardship and the fullness of the American earth. An updated version of the book was published in 1988.

Among his other books is *Arizona Wild and Free*, published by *Arizona Highways* in 1993.

Now living in Santa Fe, New Mexico, Mr. Udall continues to write, lecture, and practice environmental law.

(PRECEDING PANEL, PAGES 2-3) "Leave it as it is. You cannot improve on it. The ages have been at work on it, and man can only mar it. What you can do is to keep it for your children, your children's children, and for all who come after you, as the one great sight which every American … should see."
— President Theodore Roosevelt
at the Grand Canyon, 1903

(PRECEDING PANEL, PAGES 6-7) "On a fair morning the mountain invited you to get down and roll in its new grass and flowers. … Every living thing sang, chirped, and burgeoned … Never had there been so rare a day, or so rich a solitude to spend it in."
— Aldo Leopold,
A Sand County Almanac, 1949

(ABOVE) Sunset bestows a somber elegance on this desert scene in Catalina State Park
near Tucson at the base of Mount Lemmon.

David Muench's Arizona
Cherish The Land, Walk in Beauty

All photographs in this book were taken by David Muench. The text is the result
of collaboration between Mr. Muench and Lawrence W. Cheek.

Design: Gary Bennett
Picture Editor: Peter Ensenberger
Copy Editor: Charles Burkhart
Book Editor: Bob Albano

Prepared by the Book Division of *Arizona Highways*® magazine, a monthly
publication of the Arizona Department of Transportation.

Publisher: Nina M. La France
Managing Editor: Bob Albano
Associate Editor: Robert J. Farrell
Art Director: Mary Winkelman Velgos
Photography Director: Peter Ensenberger
Production Director: Cindy Mackey

Library of Congress Catalog Number 97-71453
ISBN 0-916179-66-4

INTRODUCTION

TEXT BY LAWRENCE W. CHEEK

Aravaipa Creek surprised the Sonoran Desert of southeastern Arizona. During a few million years the creek chiseled a secret canyon where it nourishes a renegade forest of sycamore, cottonwood, and mesquite.

We're surprised, too. For three days David Muench, his wife, Bonnie, and I have been hiking the canyon, and despite the fact that we're in the eye of the arboreal fall color riot, we haven't seen another human, a scrap of trash, or any other memorandum of civilization.

This solitude puts us in good cheer as we hike downstream to a tributary canyon David wants to photograph. Outside this sanctuary it is November 5, 1996, Election Day, and millions are stressed as they wait, argue, celebrate, or worry. Not here. Our concerns are contained and defined by the canyon. Will Bonnie and I be able to make the obsessive David pack up his camera in time to trek the four miles back to our tents before dark? If not, how curious might a mountain lion become about a shivering city boy passing the night in a pile of autumn leaves?

I'm immersed in these wilderness thoughts when the canyon's calm is shattered by man-made thunder. Two U.S. Air Force fighters streak low, no more than a thousand feet above the ground, strewing a blanket of sound that penetrates every crack and fiber in the canyon. We stand and stare after the jets, adrenaline and annoyance skirmishing inside us.

"Well," says David at last, "I feel safe *now!*" Instantly the tension dissolves. We all laugh and "forgive" the Air Force and plod on down the creek.

David, I realize, just did something with a quip that he's been doing for decades in his landscape photography. He defined a transitory moment, an instant in time when something changes.

David Muench was born to photography like a Kennedy to politics. His father, Josef Muench, was a German immigrant who began building a New World life as a landscape gardener in Santa Barbara, California, until he felt the West's grander natural landscapes tugging at him. A self-taught photographer, Josef launched a freelance business on the side. In 1938 he and *Arizona Highways* discovered each other, and the rest is photographic history. *Arizona Highways* published thousands of his images and his work appeared in 280 magazines before he stopped counting.

Born in 1936, David grew up in his father's darkroom and in wilderness campgrounds throughout Arizona and the West. He learned the basics of landscape photography from Josef and a profound curiosity and love for nature from his mother, Joyce Rockwood Muench. David declared artistic independence early on, virtually under Josef's nose. "I printed his black-and-white negatives for a long time," David once told me. "And I was expressing myself with them, putting my own stamp on them."

Writing an article about the Muench family a few years ago, I studied hundreds of Josef's and David's images and discerned something about the temperament of the men behind them. Josef's

DAVID MUENCH WAS
BORN TO PHOTOGRAPHY
LIKE A KENNEDY TO POLITICS

(LEFT) A deep, archlike opening in the canyon wall frames the Aravaipa Canyon Wilderness, a verdant ribbon nurtured by one of the last perennial streams flowing in the Sonoran Desert.

(PRECEDING PANEL) Sycamore leaves, a full-color introduction to Nature's exuberant geometry, quilt the slopes of Madera Canyon in the Mount Wrightson Wilderness in the Santa Rita Mountains south of Tucson.

landscapes were staged with immaculate precision; there was never a leaf, a cloud or a Navajo out of place. More than 40 years ago, the Annual of the Photographic Society of America described his darkroom as having "all the rigid cleanliness of a hospital operating room," and added that he "maintains the same meticulousness in the field." You could see that meticulousness in every photograph.

David's shots are just as careful, but they are less predictable, less rigid, invested with more overt drama. They exude more emotion and demand more involvement. How else to say this? Josef is German, David is American.

I understood this distinction after staring for what seemed like an hour at a black-and-white print of the White House Ruin in northeastern Arizona's Canyon de Chelly that David shot in 1968. The picture caught a transitory moment that told a sweeping story.

Before David shot, the Anasazi ruin appeared tiny and inconsequential at the foot of the immense canyon wall. He waited as the sun shopped for an opening in the afternoon clouds, and when it found one, it squinted through and spotlighted the ruin. Without the light, the building always appears humble and fragile, but in this picture it glowed with the prescient fire of human ambition.

"I want to convey what I'm feeling as well as what I'm seeing," David told me.

One of David's hallmark photographic devices is the "near-far" image that sweeps from a foreground detail — a spiky agave, a backlit sunflower, a contorted juniper — to a distant mountain horizon equally intense in its detail. Every element, nearest to farthest, will be in the same perfect focus. On one level, this simply is a way of making a vivid and dramatic picture, conveying as much information as possible. On another, it makes a philosophical statement that David believes is vitally important: all of nature is a context, each tiny element critically important to the health of the whole. Kill a flower, and the mountain on which it bloomed is diminished. Endanger a species, and you imperil a planet.

He's an environmentalist, of course — it goes with the territory of nature photography. He worries about shrinking wildernesses and metastasizing crowds, but the political and economic problems of protecting the landscapes overwhelm him. He doesn't know the answers, and after four decades of photography, he is reconciled to the fact that the only difference he can make is to document the beauty of Nature and hope we get the point. He's all too aware, of course, of the built-in environmental problem with landscape photography: if you shoot it, they will come. Keep on taking and publishing these stunning photos of Aravaipa Canyon, and more people will want to see it for themselves. Who can blame them?

(ABOVE) A transitory moment: a selective splash of sunlight probes into Canyon de Chelly to light the White House Ruin — and hint at the ambitions that would come to challenge Nature in Arizona.

(RIGHT) The desert's strangeness is exceeded only by its ferocity. To survive, everything — like the Mohave yucca in the foreground and the Joshua tree in back — is prepared to hurt any creature that gets too close. In the background, man-made Lake Mead marks the Arizona-Nevada border.

(RIGHT) Sycamore leaves float artistically in a pool of water reflecting trees and a wall of Aravaipa Canyon. **(FAR RIGHT)** David Muench works during autumn in Aravaipa Canyon with his Linhof Technika.

David has lived in Southern California all his life, but he calls Arizona his spiritual home. His artistry is rooted in photographic excursions to Arizona with his parents, and he has talked candidly about wanting to take his last walk on earth in the desert.

Why? I once questioned him intensely and came away with two critical words.

One was *silence*. When photographing the desert, David prefers to work alone. He doesn't want to talk to anyone or see anyone. The silence imposed by the landscape is to him a form of meditation that you can feel in his photographs of the desert: they are so meditative, so private, that it seems they are intended to be viewed alone. Sharing them in a crowd, chattering over them — well, that wouldn't quite be sacrilege, but it definitely would shatter the mood.

The other was *surprise*. He loves to be astonished by Nature, and Arizona — whether desert, mountain or canyon — is a funfair of creation. The light, the land forms, the tenacious struggle for life in a hostile environment all interact in unpredictable and constantly changing ways.

David's level of awareness makes him a good companion to have along on an Arizona trail; he sees more than the rest of us. A sycamore leaf left over from last season, now eroded into a gossamer skeleton of exquisite geometric finesse. An unusual lightfall on a boulder that turns something altogether common into an object of amazing beauty. The Grand Canyon probably doesn't need David Muench to demonstrate it to us, but there are 70 million more acres of Arizona that still have much to reveal. This is what keeps him coming back, obsessed with exploring every possible mood of the land.

Did I say he's obsessed?

Just off Aravaipa Creek a pool of clear, nearly still water reflects backlit sycamores and the canyon wall and blue sky behind. David jokes about being in a "reflective mood" and sets up his 4-by-5 inch

PHOTO BY LAWRENCE W. CHEEK

Linhof Technika at the pool's edge. Most of his photographs are taken with this tedious contraption — a stone ax of a camera.

He squats in the mud and begins plotting a picture. At his request, I harvest some yellow sycamore leaves that are ready to fall and bring them to him. Like a kid launching an armada of toy boats, he sails the leaves into the water and waits for the breeze to blow them into his proposed foreground. Nature, naturally, is uninterested in cooperating. The leaves drift into an inartistic pattern. Specks of foam arise on the water surface. Too much breeze moves the leaves on the trees in the background. A cirrus cloud parks in the wrong place. For two hours David floats sycamore leaves, awaiting a transitory moment.

"This is bordering on silly," he admits.

We move on to the afternoon's destination, the mouth of a tributary canyon named, rather ungraciously, Horse Camp. The way into the canyon is almost blocked by minivan-sized boulders that have somehow rolled down from the highlands, but just behind the rocks is a miniature world of fragile beauty: ephemeral pools of emerald water embraced by ferns and November wildflowers and illuminated by the low autumn sun trickling through sycamore leaves. This is the Sonoran Desert, remember — we're barely 70 miles northeast of downtown Tucson and only 300 feet higher in elevation. David is intent now, trying to coax this improbable oasis onto film before the shadows close in — and before a moonless night maroons us miles away from our tents.

I hear the shutter of his Linhof click open, then a hiss: "Damn!"

A butterfly has fluttered into his foreground, alighting on a flower for afternoon cocktails. It would make a charming video. But in the three seconds that David's 4-by-5 is open for business, the insect will record its passage as a white smudge.

But I feel it has been an interesting day: in the space of an afternoon, I have heard David Muench joke about the Air Force and curse a butterfly.

LIGHT

I love photographing in the quiet hours. Just before dawn, just after sunset, deep in fog, late on a winter afternoon with cirrus clouds filtering a sun low in the sky, or in the wake of a summer thunderstorm when the air has an unearthly stillness and the light isn't sure what it's about to become — these are my "quiet hours." These are the times that magic lives in the light.

It's a subtle form of magic, and I haven't always understood it. For a long time I wanted to shout — to create photographic spectacles with light erupting in them. I wanted every picture to surprise and astonish. This only illuminated the narrowness of my experience. Now I feel most exhilarated by more subtle effects. Light isn't an end in itself any more. It's what gives meaning to form.

John C. Van Dyke may have been the first person to understand this in relation to Arizona. He wasn't an artist, but he was an art historian, and he had the gift of great perception. In his 1901 book, *The Desert*, he explained the transforming power of light on form:

The dunes are always rhythmical and flowing in their forms; and for color the desert has nothing that surpasses them. In the early morning, before the sun is up, they are air-blue, reflecting the sky overhead; at noon they are pale lines of dazzling orange-colored light, waving and undulating in the heated air; at sunset they are often flooded with a rose or mauve color; under a blue moonlight they shine white as icebergs in the northern seas.

Almost three-quarters of a century later, writer Edward Abbey, in his classic *Desert Solitaire*, tried to describe the effects of light on the mood of the land:

Despite its clarity and simplicity, however, the desert wears at the same time, paradoxically, a veil of mystery. Motionless and silent it evokes in us an elusive hint of something unknown, unknowable, about to be revealed. Since the desert does not act it seems to be waiting — but waiting for what?

> LIGHT GIVES MEANING TO FORM. FOR ME, LIGHT IS THE ULTIMATE AFFIRMATION OF LIFE.

I feel this "hint of something unknown, unknowable" most profoundly in the subtlest light. Fog, for example. Saguaros and chollas (creatures that have no idea what they're doing in the fog!) trudge up a desert hillside, each one appearing in the receding distance less substantial, less real. They seem to be in the process of becoming something other than what they are, but becoming what? Because of the fog, the answer is unknown and unknowable.

A lot of people (including some photographers) sulk and stay inside when rain falls on the land. For me, this is when the landscape glows. It's transformed. I've spent whole days while rain fell on and off, climbing around on metamorphic rock and photographing in the intervals between the showers. It's like putting the whole scene in a gemstone tumbler and polishing it.

Backlighting is an old story in photography, but when I work in Arizona I'm continually being revitalized by its possibilities. There's the bold, dramatic backlight, of course, when you catch the low

(RIGHT) The fine, ruddy sand of the Chinle Valley on the Navajo Reservation in northeastern Arizona reflects not only the whims of the wind but also the continuously changing colors and moods of sun and sky.

(FOLLOWING PANEL) In the desert, even dust can be a photographer's friend: here it forms an amber scrim tinting the thorn forest of Tucson Mountain Park, while a glowing armature of backlight surrounds each saguaro.

morning sun behind a crowd of chollas and they become a forest of glowing, cactus-shaped halos. But you can also take a composition of simple, ordinary elements — a boulder and a tuft of wild grass — and subtle backlight will reveal the most wonderful forms and textures in it. Light redefines the familiar, and turns it into something exotic.

Reflected light can create magical transformations. In late fall, when the cottonwoods and sycamores turn in the desert canyons, the riparian canopy will harvest the sunlight, churn it around in the leaves, and throw it back out at the canyon walls with a subtle gold or amber tint. Reflected light colors everything it strikes, transforming the whole character of the landscape.

This idea of character or mood has everything to do with light.

I was once showing a friend two photographs of Anasazi petroglyphs on sandstone near the Little Colorado River. One photo had an orange cast because it was taken right at sunset. The other had shifted into violet because it was about 15 minutes after sunset. My friend said that the orange photo suggested a prehistoric civilization at a volatile transition in time — a people in the process of becoming something. (What they became, unfortunately, was extinct!) The violet photo, he said, hinted at something timeless — suggesting that the spirit of the Anasazi had always existed and would always exist.

I hadn't imagined this story line when I was taking the photographs, and I think it's debatable. But it demonstrates very dramatically how light not only alters our perception of physical objects, but also colors our emotions about them.

Joseph Campbell said in *The Power of Myth* that people aren't so much seeking the meaning of life, but simply "the experience of being alive." I feel that I've enjoyed this experience many times, and when I look back, light usually defines the moment. For me, light is the ultimate affirmation of life.

I was hiking through Aravaipa Canyon in the fall when I stumbled onto three mature sycamores on the south side of the creek. Direct light was scarce at this time of year; these trees wouldn't have enjoyed more than a couple of hours a day. The southern sun hugged the white bark of the trunks, trying to claim them for the light. But the other side, the shadow, attracted me. It wasn't a mute black shadow. It incorporated the light reflected from a creek, a riparian forest and a desert canyon wall. The whole life of this canyon was wrapped up in the soft shadow on this sycamore trunk.

Another time, I was working in the Lukachukai Mountains on the Navajo Reservation. I had had a great afternoon shooting, and all of a sudden the full moon rose over the mountains. I had forgotten it was coming, and I thought, "Oh my God, something more!"

In a few minutes there was this wonderful transition, the amber sun dying and handing over the landscape to the care of the brittle white moon. It was an epic drama of light, played out in the space of just a couple of minutes.

There's never a shortage of drama in the landscape of Arizona. But the quiet hours seem to have the best lines.

PORTFOLIO

(LEFT) A pool in the West Fork of Oak Creek near Sedona reflects a profusion of autumn color and a mood of profound tranquillity.

(RIGHT) Monument Valley challenges every photographer to discover some fresh image, to interpret its great geologic sculptures in some new light. That is always the key — light — as in this brittle January sunrise behind Ye'i Bichai Rocks.

(FAR RIGHT) If the muddy runoff from recent rains has not reddened it, the Little Colorado River often runs a brilliant azure with the calcium carbonate-rich water from Blue Spring. Blue Moon Bench provides this view near the Little Colorado's confluence with the Colorado River.

(RIGHT) Fog is not just a meteorological phenomenon. It also simulates a mood. In the desert, fog falls over the land like a blanket of uncanny silence. Among these sandstone domes in the Paria Canyon-Vermilion Cliffs Wilderness, it is as if the world — just for a moment — has ceased to breathe.

(LEFT) Nature's eternal constant is change: The Lukachukai dunes and the buttes on the Navajo Reservation are composed of the same sand, and both are being resculpted by wind and water — the dunes over the space of a day, the buttes across geologic eons.

LIGHT

(FOLLOWING PANEL) The peculiar geometry of the desert — here fashioned by spidery ocotillo and rain-fattened saguaro — intensifies under the sun's backlighting at Saguaro National Park in Tucson.

(RIGHT) Even in the cool high country, water is precious in Arizona. This tiny cascade on Fossil Creek below the Mogollon Rim will find its way to the Verde River, which helps slake Phoenix's thirst.

(FAR RIGHT) Fossil Springs, the basis of a wilderness area, is the originating source of Fossil Creek.

(PAGE 136) Like eye holes in a giant's mask, these sandstone windows peer across the desert at the red rocks of the Sedona area.

(PAGE 137) October's reflections introduce seasonal color to a quiet pool in the West Fork of Oak Creek.

(LEFT) A full moon rises over Wotan's Throne (left) and Vishnu Temple, its crisp silver light beginning to replace the rich red and violet of the evening sun in the Grand Canyon.

(FAR LEFT) Although it forces a worrisome problem onto the Grand Canyon, man-made haze creates dimensions in light. Here in Granite Gorge, the silvery Colorado River dominates the landscape, while the ridges in the background become two-dimensional cutouts, all but fading together in their slight tonal differences.

(LEFT) One of the wonders of the Southwest's sunlight manifests itself by slashing through a rift in the clouds and spotlighting a piece of the landscape. Here, showing off its versatility, the sun burns red on a palisade of the Lukachukai Mountains on the Navajo Reservation and amber on the rocks in the foreground.

(FAR LEFT) Selective light can also highlight unusual geometric form, like these bread loaf-shaped boulders overlooking the Colorado River just above Lava Falls.

35

(RIGHT) "It is no place for flowers," naturalist John C. Van Dyke wrote of the desert in 1901. That observation meant only that he had passed through after a dry winter. If soaking winter rain falls at least once every two weeks, April will explode in floral color, such as these Mexican poppies in the Sonoran Desert's Altar Valley west of Tucson.

(FAR RIGHT) Another Van Dyke observation — "Ridge upon ridge melts into the distant sky in lines of lilac and purple" — describes perfectly this sunset view of the Gila Bend Mountains in west-central Arizona.

(LEFT) Limestone rimrock in the shadowed foreground looks as white as frost, while Zoroaster and Brahma temples glow with crimson evening light across the Grand Canyon's chasm.

(FAR LEFT) The swirling and cascading water of Oak Creek reflects a rosy sunrise — another example of the color and mood of the sky changing the character of the landscape.

(FOLLOWING PANEL) Travertine ledges form miniature cascades in the sediment-rich Little Colorado River near Blue Springs.

LIGHT

(LEFT) For just a few moments each day, the sun visits this narrow slot in the Permian sandstone at Toroweap Point on the Grand Canyon's North Rim.

(FAR LEFT) "At length, as the sun draws near the horizon," wrote the poetic geologist Clarence Dutton of the Grand Canyon, "the great drama of the day begins." Each day brings a new script with the changing interplay of sunlight, clouds, air, and the season. The Canyon seems eternal, and yet it is always changing.

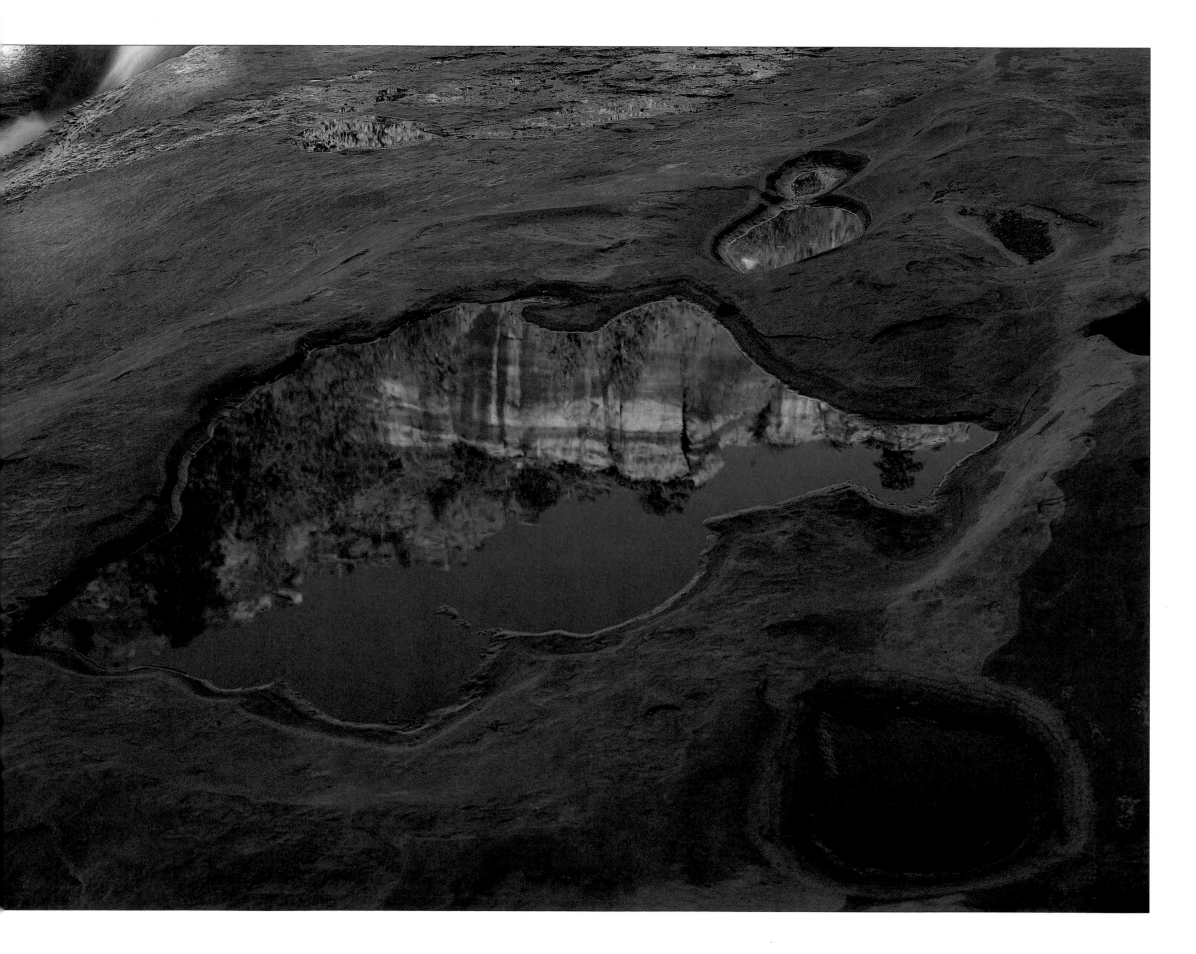

(LEFT) On a cloudless day in the Sonoran Desert the windows of opportunity for artistic photography may be very narrow — two or three minutes at sunrise and sunset — but those windows reveal color and form unlike anywhere else in the world.

(FAR LEFT) Sandstone is a geological chameleon; it assumes different colors with changes in the angle and character of the light striking it. The sunlit walls of Oak Creek Canyon reflected in the pool are a brilliant orange, while the shaded sandstone cradling the water is a velvety mauve — for the moment.

(RIGHT) Golden aspen leaves over Bright Angel Canyon on the North Rim of the Grand Canyon celebrate the bright autumn sun.
(FAR RIGHT) A March morning's sunrise at Yavapai Point on the Canyon's South Rim exudes a quality of warmth despite a frosting of snow.
(FOLLOWING PANEL) Mount Graham, literally basking in the sun, rises 10,717 feet over the Gila River Valley in southeastern Arizona.

(RIGHT) A grove of teddy bear cholla, resplendent in its prodigious cutlery, flirts with a low sun in the Kofa National Wildlife Refuge near Yuma.

(FAR RIGHT) Sedona's signature scene centers on Cathedral Rock as it is seen from Oak Creek's Red Rock Crossing. But the ever-changing light always makes new images possible.

FORM

"I have long been an admirer of the octopus," wrote Loren Eiseley in *The Immense Journey*. "It gives one a feeling of confidence to see Nature still busy with experiments … "

Eiseley's essays on nature have exerted a profound influence on me. His thoughts about the octopus and experiments, oddly enough, resonate with me when I'm photographing Arizona. The forms of the land and its life are so strange, so mysterious.

I'm always drawn to dunes, for example. I could do a whole book on dunes alone. A dune is ephemeral, a creation of one moment in time, but the form, the surface design, the light, and the mood are constantly in transition.

There are as many surface patterns in dunes as there are rhythms in music. The ripples on the surface can seem urgent or merely busy, confused or perfectly tranquil, jagged or gently flowing. The angle of the slope and the way the sunlight is hitting them add complexities. A low, strong sun can create miniature shadows under the breakers that give the whole composition a crisp, precise character. A higher sun filtered through thin cirrus clouds can make any dunescape seem soft and lazy.

WHEN YOU PHOTOGRAPH A DUNE, YOU CAPTURE FOREVER A FORM THAT WILL EXIST FOR ONLY A MOMENT. FOR ME, THAT'S A VERY POWERFUL ACT.

Goethe said architecture is "frozen music." I imagine he was thinking of classical music. Dunes, to me, are an eternal jazz festival, an improvisation that never ends. When you photograph one, you capture forever a form that will exist for only a moment. For me, that's a very powerful act.

The sandstone forms of Northern Arizona are geologic relatives of the dunes, but the time frame is different. They're being sculpted across centuries, not minutes, and the process creates even more fantastic, grotesque forms. You can lose yourself in them, mentally and literally.

Slot canyons such as Antelope Canyon and Paria Canyon are sandstone worlds unto themselves. Nothing in your experiences anywhere else prepares you for them. For that reason, many photographs of slot canyons look like pure abstractions. Big, flowing, convoluting forms swirl and billow and mingle and collide, and because it's all created by the friction of water rushing through these deep, narrow slots (which can be 400 feet deep and three feet wide), all the surfaces are smooth and graceful.

But this form is deceptive. A friend was looking at some of my

(RIGHT) Flash floods have sculpted the soft Navajo sandstone of Antelope Canyon into complex, convoluted forms. Sunlight streaming into a slot canyon, however, isn't necessarily a guarantee of safety from raging waters. Distant thunderstorms on the canyon's watershed can send a flood racing through without notice.

(FOLLOWING PANEL) In Arizona, Nature herself appears to create cairns through the capricious process of erosion. The Lukachukai Mountains in northeastern Arizona lay out the backdrop for these alluvial boulders.

photographs of Buckskin Gulch, and he sensed a very different character: "It looks *ominous*," he said. He was right; it is an ominous environment. Hike the canyon floor, and every few yards you'll look up and see logs wedged in the walls 30 feet over your head. You'll remember that what put them there was the latest flood that flashed through the canyon. Anyone there during the next flash flood would be unlucky.

This is what's so captivating about the forms of Arizona. There's this incredible duality of character. Something that appears beautiful and serene and benign is prepared to use deadly force on you, and will have no trace of regret after doing so. It's very humbling.

There is an infinite variety of ways that an artist can use form. But the more powerful the form, the more it will agree with abstraction. For example, I've photographed Monument Valley under the most unlikely condition imaginable: a howling dust storm. It blew every bit of color and detail out of the landscape and left nothing but the fuzzy outlines of those great monoliths against the sky — and because all the detail was gone, the forms seemed to acquire even more power. (They looked ominous!) I've also photographed Monument Valley with an extreme wide-angle lens in the last seconds of a dramatic sunset, shrinking the big rocks into small black silhouettes propped up on the horizon. You can't tell what they are — and that heightens the mystery around them.

Powerful form exists everywhere in Arizona, not just in mountains and canyons.

I was studying a Petrified Forest log that had collected rain water in little pits in its stone bark. Late in the afternoon, they became little pools of a deep, intense blue. Another transitory moment, another entry in the catalog of infinite possibilities.

Speaking of infinite possibilities, I spotted an "octopus" during a recent visit to Arizona: the root system of a giant cottonwood growing on a desert river bank. Exposed by the erosion of many floods, the roots appeared like huge tentacles that were wrapped around each other, around clumps of dirt, even around boulders that had been washed downstream into their grasp. Ancient, gnarly, and mysterious, the roots looked like nothing else in the desert. They seemed like the product of Nature still busy experimenting with the form of a tree — and maybe that's exactly how to account for this shape: an experiment in how to cling to life in a challenging environment.

I thought of Loren Eiseley. Seeing Nature so busy experimenting with survival gave me a feeling of confidence.
It affirmed: Life will abide.

PORTFOLIO

(LEFT) A lithic junkyard from the age of dinosaurs, the shattered landscape of the Petrified Forest exhibits a gallery of organized forms in the rings of ancient trees.

(RIGHT) I like to use the term "petrified sand form" to describe parallel ripples such as this creation of wind and water in the Paria Canyon-Vermilion Cliffs Wilderness. **(FAR RIGHT)** Sweeping over a rain pool, these salmon-colored striations of the Vermilion Cliffs resemble a solidified sea of rolling dunes — which is precisely what they are.

(RIGHT) Elements formed the walls of Antelope Canyon like a meringue of sandstone, scooping, curling, peaking, and rolling with incredible grace and complexity. Yet, they are temporary forms of beauty — the elements will change them.
(FAR RIGHT) Sandstone slabs love to self-destruct into arches and windows. This view in the Paria Canyon-Vermilion Cliffs Wilderness takes in three openings.Look thoroughly and you'll locate the third opening.

(RIGHT) "This is the land of gods in exile," wrote Arizona poet Richard Shelton of another desert to the south. But his description also evokes the spiritual dimension of Monument Valley in Navajo Tribal Park.

(LEFT) "Secret places deep in the canyons, known only to the deer and the coyotes and the dragon-flies," wrote naturalist Edward Abbey, describing the lifesaving rain pools such as this one in Waterholes Canyon.

(LEFT) The business of Nature can cast remarkable geometric exhibitions. Here, hedgehog cactuses defend their delicate blooms with an arsenal of pointed threats.

(FAR LEFT) More of the business of Nature: As if in prayer, these aspens stretch toward the light over the San Francisco Mountains in the Kachina Peaks Wilderness, an area deemed sacred by Navajo and Hopi people.

(RIGHT) Great sandstone slabs accent the high desert plateau in the Kachina Peaks Wilderness. They are framing snow-capped Humphreys Peak, a volcano whose last eruptions were about 200,000 years ago.
(FAR RIGHT) Thousands of little-known geologic oddments exist on the vast Navajo Nation. These sandstone skyscrapers rise amid low mesas near Lukachukai Creek.

(LEFT) Summer grass at Hawley Lake weaves into its own reflection, creating a delightful geometry in the land of the White Mountain Apaches.

(FAR LEFT) Long after the spring runoff from the White Mountains has subsided, the Black River pools itself into a reflective mood.

(RIGHT) Window Rock is a nearly perfect circular puncture in a formation on the Defiance Plateau near the Navajo Nation capital of the same name.

(FAR RIGHT) Now punctuated with monoliths, Monument Valley was once a solid sandstone plateau as high as the tallest buttes and spires stand today. The plateau crumbled away into huge splinters and slabs like these in the foreground. In back stand the "Three Sisters," still slimming down as the wind and water reshape them grain by grain.

(RIGHT) Roughly rounded forms of alluvial boulders contrast with the squarely chiseled Lukachukai Buttes in the background.
(FAR RIGHT) Alternately soft and brittle, sandstone can erode into shapes that seem to defy both logic and gravity, like Cobra Arch in the Paria Canyon-Vermilion Cliffs Wilderness.

(LEFT) The soft, gentle light of a May dawn reveals the geology of Marble Canyon in more elegant detail than possible in the direct sun of midday. FORM

(FAR LEFT) The capricious Colorado River doubles back on itself at Horseshoe Bend, leaving a rocky peninsula in Glen Canyon.

(RIGHT) "A nursery of great silence," essayist Page Stegner said of Canyon Country, a description that captures the mood of a drift through Marble Canyon, precursor to the Grand Canyon. **(FAR RIGHT)** "All the scenic features of this cañon land are on a giant scale, strange and weird," reported Grand Canyon pioneer John Wesley Powell. For anyone seeing the Canyon it for the first time today, it remains an exploration of an alien world.

(RIGHT) A sliver of a summer cumulus skyscape appears through White Mesa Arch on the Kaibito Plateau in Navajo land.
(FAR RIGHT) Fire colors of morning sun striking White Mesa Arch contrast vividly with the last remnants of a February snowstorm.

(RIGHT) Where water runs in the mountains and canyons of Arizona, it leaves an exhibition of sculpture beside it. This tiny cascade is on Fish Creek in the Superstition Wilderness east of Phoenix.
(FAR RIGHT) Kaibito Creek on the Navajo Reservation makes a little-known "horseshoe" in Chaol Canyon.

(LEFT) A pool in the Pajarito Wilderness of Southern Arizona's Coronado National Forest reflects a dark sapphire sky and a tree undressed for the winter.

(FAR LEFT) A sandstone boulder struggles to hold onto a precarious perch, and a stunted juniper forces its way into cracks for nourishment near the Lukachukai Mountains. In the background, a low sun illuminates Gregg Arch.

(RIGHT) Since prehistoric times, the rain pools of southwestern Arizona's Tinajas Altas (Spanish for High Tanks) Mountains have served travelers across the desert, but the natural water containers are not always full. Hence the fatalistic Spanish name for this passage, El Camino del Diablo — The Devil's Highway.

(FAR RIGHT) The Petrified Forest is a dry, mile-high desert, but its palette of colors is endless. The conical "tepee" formations in the background are tinted by deposits of iron and manganese, giving the area its name — Blue Mesa.

LIFE

The forms of living things provide an endless source of fascination because they're forever changing. Change arrives with the light, with the seasons, with the cycles of death and rebirth, and with the endless struggle to maintain and perpetuate life.

Arizona is a miraculous place to observe all this because it's a land of such extremes, such strangeness. Abbey wrote about "the power of the odd and unexpected to startle the senses and surprise the mind out of [its] ruts of habit." I experience that power in Arizona as the incredible strategies that things adopt to survive constantly bump me out of those ruts.

The Sonoran Desert is the most lush, most varied, most dramatic desert on Earth. Sometimes I think I should be covering Australia or some other exotic place, just to stuff as many experiences into my short life as I can. But a trip into the Sonoran Desert is always enough to pull me back into the reality of my neighborhood. The new experiences are right here.

I traveled through the Sonoran Desert in the spring of 1996 after one of the driest winters in decades. It displayed a mood I had never experienced before — parched, seared, hostile. I had the sensation that every living thing in that community was locked in a desperate fight to survive, and that somehow my presence disrupted that effort. I had to get out of there. Eight months later I was back. The fall rains had come, and the desert exhibited an entirely different character. Wildflowers were blooming. Since March hadn't been productive, Nature simply declared a November "spring."

I looked at a prickly pear that had rooted about 12 feet over my head in the notch of a huge cottonwood's trunk and felt amazement at the genius of life. At one point during a hike through a desert canyon, I could see three distinct biotic communities — a riparian woodland, a piñon-juniper forest, and desert scrub. They thrived next to each other just because the canyon changed direction, creating three patterns of sun and rain.

The "sky islands" in the Sonoran Desert — the mountain ranges that thrust upward eight thousand feet and higher from the desert floor — conjure inspiration for me.

Joseph Campbell said in *The Power of Myth* that we all need a sacred place, a temple for meditation in nature — "a place where you can simply experience and bring forth what you are and what you might be … the place of creative incubation." These mountain islands, so isolated from each other and from the desert from which they spring, are such places for me.

To reach any of the summits, you have to climb through five or six biological zones, so you sense cycles of conflict and resolution as you climb. And then at the top, you're beset by this intangible quality of solitude. You're visiting a self-contained, self-sufficient world, a place where a subspecies of squirrel has evolved into something different from its relatives on a mountain 30 miles away. For me, this affirms the persistence of life.

For years, the Apaches have been fighting against development of observatories on one of these sky islands, Mount Graham near Safford. They see it as a sacred place. Without taking sides, I'll just say that a permanent human presence in a place seldom enhances its sacredness.

> I OFTEN WONDER: WITH ALL OUR TECHNOLOGY, HAVE WE REALLY LEARNED ANYTHING ABOUT NATURE EXCEPT HOW TO SUPPRESS IT?

(RIGHT) Even though the symbols are cryptic, panels of petroglyphs such as these in Monument Valley give us a sense of connection to the personalities who lived in centuries past.

(FOLLOWING PANEL) The sun, wrote naturalist John C. Van Dyke in *The Desert* in 1901, "is the one supreme beauty to which all things pay allegiance." This sunrise fires up the Pinaleno Mountains, which Apaches revere.

I rarely include any evidence of human presence in my landscapes, unless it's a human form for the sake of scale. I don't have any great interest in photographing buildings or cities — unless they're at least 800 years old.

When I look at ruins like White House in Canyon de Chelly or Crack-in-Rock at Wupatki, I'm stunned by their perfect simplicity. That's not a patronizing judgment; it's a profound compliment. These buildings exist in perfect harmony with their environment. They give no offense. They appear to grow out of the land, as if their architects had somehow tapped into the consciousness of Nature.

If they had, one of the reasons would be purely practical. The prehistoric Pueblo people of the Southwest — the Anasazi, Sinagua, Mogollon and Salado — had no wheels or draft animals, so they had to create their buildings with the materials at hand. On the Colorado Plateau, this usually meant sandstone, which is soft enough to be easily shaped into masonry blocks, and red clay mortar to hold the blocks together. So a cliff dwelling would be made of the same stuff as the cliff itself. The architecture was a slight rearrangement of the landscape rather than an exhibition of foreign products.

But a lot of people see more than this practical reason, and this must be why I find myself being drawn back to these ruins to photograph them again and again. Vincent Scully, the prominent architecture historian, wrote:

> They are nature, pure and simple, but their resemblance to the shapes of the earth is not accidental entirely either. It is … at once an act of reverence and a natural congruence between two natural things.

An act of reverence. I love that idea, because it's so dramatically opposite of what we 20th-century humans do to the land. We seize it, we control it, we mine it, we reshape it, we impose cities on it without any thought of respect or harmony. I often wonder: with all our technology, have we really learned anything about Nature except how to suppress it?

I believe that because the prehistoric Americans didn't have much technology they had to discover a different reality. They had no way of understanding climate cycles, and they couldn't freeze leftover turkey for next week's meals, so they developed some very strong spiritual links to Nature, encouraging them to trust it and allowing them to survive in it. I think it was very real for them, and that it worked for them for thousands of years. It may have stopped working because their sheer numbers finally overwhelmed the land, or because they stopped believing in those acts of reverence.

Some Navajos today express the belief that their predecessors, the Anasazi, died out or scattered because they became too ambitious, and that disrupted *hózhó*, or balance, in their world. I can certainly see that possibility in the ruins. The biggest pueblos, the most ambitious building projects — most of them came just before the abandonment.

There are some ruins in the Southwest where the people seemed to be putting on a spectacle. Mesa Verde in Colorado and Chaco Canyon in New Mexico, come quickly to anyone's mind. Their architecture is magnificent, but to me there's something more poignant and somehow more inspiring about the more modest ruins. They exist in perfect harmony with the land, revering it rather than challenging it.

We could do worse — and we have.

PORTFOLIO

(LEFT) Lonely Lomaki, one of some 2,000 Sinagua ruins in Wupatki National Monument north of Flagstaff, was occupied only for about 100 years around the 12th century A.D. Its sandstone masonry flows so organically from the land that it presages Frank Lloyd Wright's credo: "A house should not be *on* a hill, but *of* it."

(LEFT) Kokopelli, the humpbacked flutist who lately performs on earrings and napkin holders, here dances across the lower end of a sandstone boulder above the Little Colorado River in an authentic Anasazi rendering. The precise meaning that the character held for prehistoric peoples may never be known.
(RIGHT) Anasazi handprints on a sandstone slab reach across the centuries. Many archaeologists believe they served as a kind of signature, perhaps to accompany prayer requests.

(LEFT) Prickly pear, the most tenacious and adaptable plant of Arizona and possibly everywhere else, is discouraged by nothing — not even this "soil" consisting of crumbled volcanic lava in the Sycamore Canyon Wilderness west of Sedona.

(RIGHT) Prehistoric Sinagua ruins, mostly hidden from easy view, occupy many natural alcoves of the canyon walls of the Red Rock-Secret Mountain Wilderness north of Sedona. Whether these improbable aeries were selected because they were easy to defend has been debated by archaeologists for the last hundred years.

(LEFT) A life-sustaining artery —
a wash, seasonal creek, or
perennial stream — usually
traces the floor of every desert
canyon. Here Kaibito Creek
cascades over sandstone
ledges in Chaol Canyon on the
Navajo Reservation.

(RIGHT) We can only guess at
the reasons, but prehistoric
cultures seemed to designate
certain desert hills and canyon
walls as bulletin boards or
communal galleries. This
prolific Hohokam petroglyph
site is at Painted Rocks on the
Gila River.

98

(LEFT) Forests punctuate even the very dry Mohave Desert. This spiny thicket of Joshua trees (Yucca brevifolia) is near Grand Wash Cliffs by Lake Mead.

(RIGHT) For reasons of their own, some plants choose solitude. This teddy bear cholla goes it alone near Courthouse Butte in the Eagletail Mountain Wilderness northeast of Yuma.

LIFE

99

(LEFT) Dirt trapped in a fissure provides enough sustenance for life on the rocky bank of the Colorado River flowing over the desert floor of the Grand Canyon. **(RIGHT)** The Grand Canyon also shelters signs of human life. Evidently intended to communicate across the centuries, ambitious pictographs are found on rocks or cliffs tucked away from the sun and rain.

(LEFT) Easily spooked and threatened by expanding human activities, the wary desert bighorn is only rarely sighted in the Grand Canyon.
(RIGHT) Ferns luxuriate in a trickling waterfall in the Grand Canyon's Elf's Chasm.

103

(BELOW) Rock art may have been a prehistoric *lingua franca* to communicate ideas about rain, hunting, and fertility. This site, along the Gila River east of Yuma, is believed to have been a gathering place for sacred ceremonies centuries ago.

(RIGHT) Here at Council Rocks, Apache people led by Cochise and the U.S. government represented by Gen. Otis Howard reached a treaty in 1872. The military had found this area — now called Cochise Stronghold — impregnable, and that's why the Indians often hid there during their guerrilla warfare.

Desert inhabitants sometimes
seek the protection of fellow
plants in their fight to survive
in a harsh environment.
(LEFT) A flowering staghorn
cholla embraces an agave's
crisp green daggers in the
Chiricahua Mountains.
(RIGHT) A hedgehog cactus
blooms in the protective lee
of a paloverde trunk in the
Superstition Wilderness.

(BELOW) Mystifying basketmaker pictographs near Ear Cave in the Navajo Reservation's Canyon de Chelly depict ornamented human forms with what appear to be trumpets and sound-wave symbols protruding from their heads and left ears. Archaeologists think they may represent a deity, but this is only conjecture.

(RIGHT) A protective overhang preserves these cliff dwellings above Chinle Wash, also on Navajo land. The Anasazi abandoned the area in the late 13th century A.D., coinciding with the great drought of 1279-1299.

(LEFT) A creek in the Santa Rita Mountains south of Tucson nourishes a colorful sycamore grove in Madera Canyon.

(RIGHT) A line of linked figures with head ornaments in Canyon de Chelly possibly represents ceremonial dancing.

(FOLLOWING PANEL) Lomaki Ruin in Wupatki National Monument looks out at majestic Humphreys Peak near Flagstaff. The peak is the residence of the modern Hopis' kachina spirits, and logically a place of spiritual significance to their ancestral prehistoric Sinagua people as well.

(LEFT) In a good spring, Mexican poppies carpet the foothills of the Ajo Mountains in Organ Pipe National Monument along the Mexican border.

(RIGHT) In all the continent there may be no more distinctive a silhouette than the Sonoran Desert's saguaro cactus. This one houses a nest for a hawk and its mate.

(FOLLOWING PANEL) Weathered gray textures of an abandoned corral and loading chute blend into the arid grasslands of the Kanab Plateau in the remote Arizona Strip. The Shinarump Cliffs stretch along the horizon.

ECOLOGY

If I were 30 again, maybe I would feel differently. Maybe I would do something radical.

I'm about to photograph the rippled sand in Coral Pink Sand Dunes State Park. It's in Utah, but I'm looking right over the Kaibab Plateau into Arizona. The evening sun's shadows are beginning to define the wind's waves on the dunes, the color of the sand is shifting from amber to magenta, and the air is beginning to cool.

All this is an invitation to make great pictures. And it's also an invitation for the off-road vehicle crowd to roll out and tear over the dunes. They come suddenly over the hills, and there must be a dozen of them. They sound like buzz saws, carving up the landscape all around me.

Another day. I'm in the Superstition Mountains, east of Phoenix, photographing a volcanic arch. This landscape won't accommodate wheels, so I'm alone for the evening. But it's not as if I'm the first to find this place. All around me the ground is littered with bullet casings.

In the dunes, I feel outrage, but I don't act. The emotion doesn't find a way through my skin. There's a wall of resignation that contains it. I walk until I find a place that hasn't been disturbed by the drivers and photograph it.

In the Superstitions, I just feel that, well, litter is a reality of modern life. I set up my camera, comb the foreground for the casings, and toss them out of the picture.

So far, I still seem to be able to portray a pristine world on film — even if it doesn't look that way in real life. But doing so is becoming harder and harder, and that fills me with sadness.

If I were 30 again, maybe I would choose to make a statement, like David Brower or Edward Abbey. Maybe I would begin to use my photography as a political force.

But maybe not. After all, I was 30 once, and it wasn't as if the environment hadn't yet been disturbed. I'm not wild-eyed; I don't go out looking for fights. I search for harmony in things. I try to bring opposites together. That's a lot of what my photography is about.

And I can't bring myself to view environmental issues only in black and white. In between the poles stir shades of moral and ethical grays.

I respect and identify very closely with the Navajo Night Chant, a nine-day ritual of healing. Near the end, the chant says:

> With beauty before me, I walk.
> With beauty behind me, I walk.
> With beauty below me, I walk.
> With beauty above me, I walk.
> With beauty all around me, I walk.

This is what I've done all my life. I walk in beauty, I photograph in beauty, I drive in beauty, I live in beauty. Who am I to say that other people can't walk in beauty in ways different from mine? How can I say that everybody must relate to Nature just as I do?

Like any self-respecting environmentalist, I clench my fists and teeth every time I hear someone say "Glen Canyon Dam." I wish the Colorado still were a wild river. But I can't make myself condemn someone for enjoying a weekend on a houseboat on the lake that dam created. Maybe that can be a "drift in beauty" for some. I can't attack someone for buying an acre of pristine desert full of saguaros and coyotes in the Catalina Foothills of Tucson and building a house on it. I would gladly do the same.

I've often visualized that at the end of my life, I would like to walk up a desert arroyo — take that last walk with desert beauty all around me — but to do that, perhaps I'd be living there — owning an acre,

I SEARCH FOR HARMONY IN THINGS. I TRY TO BRING OPPOSITES TOGETHER. THAT'S A LOT OF WHAT MY PHOTOGRAPHY IS ABOUT.

(RIGHT) In a state pressured by rapid growth, wild places survive only with our commitment. We need places like this fern grove along the West Fork of the Colorado River in the Mount Baldy Wilderness. They help us maintain a sense of harmony and beauty.

(FOLLOWING PANEL) In the wild, the fragile can thrive in the company of the strong. Here, an evanescent moonflower (or sacred datura) blossoms in the crack of a sandstone wall in Waterholes Canyon.

living on it, altering it to suit my needs and desires.

We can't have it all. There aren't enough acres of pristine desert for everyone to have his own. There is no way to preserve the integrity of a wilderness and throw it open to hunting and logging. I can't walk down a desert arroyo if somebody is tearing along it in an off-road vehicle. Each of us will ruin the experience for the other.

What do we do? Proceed, I guess, in the way democracies must: through noisy, messy, imperfect compromise. We need to try to work out a way that protects Nature as much as possible, given all our conflicting demands on it.

While I've chosen not to shout, I am making quiet statements with my art.

What I hope that these pictures say is that we *need* wilderness. We need wild places where we will not see houses, cars, fences, signs, bullet casings, or even trails. We need places where there is no trace of human interference, because these places will then serve as a standard. We need these places because they cleanse us. Whatever pressures and frustrations we have in our lives in the cities, we can lose them out there. When we walk in beauty, all the garbage in our lives disappears.

I have no idea how to politically engineer this thought into reality, but this is what I believe: the more wilderness, the better.

In Arizona, like everywhere else in the West, the existence of wildness — let alone government-designated wilderness — is under assault. The Arizona Game and Fish Department announced in the fall of 1996 that it can't find any more bighorn sheep on Pusch Ridge, which is virtually encircled now by Tucson. The herd couldn't deal with the stress of city life. The last grizzly in Arizona died 60 years ago from a hunter's bullet. Ecologists estimate that 90 percent of Arizona's riparian environments have been lost or degraded since ranching, mining, and city living came to Arizona. Whether you're a professional environmentalist or a truck driver, I don't think you can look at these trends without sadness and alarm.

There's so little real wilderness left that we have to create "natural" environments in our cities so our kids won't completely miss it. I don't think the zoo and arboretum experience is an adequate substitute for Nature. It's too small, too sanitary, too safe. It doesn't give you a sense of the awesome power and beauty of the real thing. As Abbey said, it's not a legitimate wilderness unless there's something in it that can eat you.

And unless future generations acquire that sense of the whole thing, they won't be good stewards of it. They won't understand how it works.

But I'm a photographer, not a preacher. I say what I can with my pictures and quote the words of people who are more articulate than I am.

The words that best express the way I feel came from Chief Seattle. In 1853 the U.S. Government inquired about buying the Suquamish tribe's land, and Seattle dictated an environmental manifesto in reply. In it, he said:

> This we know: the earth does not belong to man, man belongs to the earth. All things are connected like the blood that unites us all. Man did not weave the web of life, he is merely a strand in it. Whatever he does to the web, he does to himself.

That really says it all, doesn't it?

PORTFOLIO

(LEFT) In the Red Rock-Secret Mountain Wilderness, the West Fork of Oak Creek flows through one of Arizona's most spectacular small canyons. Hikers enjoy wonderful experiences in it, but solitude no longer is among them.

(PAGE 124) A natural bridge in the Superstition Mountains' Hewett Canyon frames a landscape of dense upper Sonoran Desert growth.

(PAGE 125) Craggy, scenic peaks in the Superstition Wilderness are accessible to people only with hard work.

(LEFT) The trail to Seven Falls northeast of Tucson is an easy four miles along the flat floor of Bear Canyon — when the falls are dry. When the falls are flowing, hikers wade across a swift, cold stream — 14 times — to view the spectacular sight.

(FAR LEFT) The waterfalls and wildflowers return to Romero Canyon every spring, but the bighorn sheep have disappeared with the pressure from nearby sprawling Tucson.

(PAGE 128) The Chiricahua Mountains, tucked away in the far southeastern corner of Arizona, remain relatively unspoiled.

(PAGE 129) The forested mountain ranges of southern Arizona, 7,000 to nearly 11,000 feet high, are literally "sky islands" supporting biotic communities entirely different from the desert below — and sometimes different from each other as well. Here autumn parades through rocky Cave Creek Canyon in the Chiricahuas.

ECOLOGY

(**LEFT**) The Hellsgate Gorge is choked with giant boulders, somber evergreens, and bristling cactus. Tonto Creek flows off the Mogollon Rim through the gorge, around which a wilderness area was desingnated.

(**FAR LEFT**) "No photograph," wrote journalist Charles Lummis in 1892 upon his visit to Tonto Natural Bridge, "can give more than a hint of its appalling majesty." Today's photographs give more than a hint — they remind that the "majesty," embracing the bridge and its environs, is fragile and its preservation vital.

(**PAGE 132**) The Tule Mountains form a barren backdrop to the thorn desert in the Cabeza Prieta National Wildlife Refuge.

(**PAGE 133**) Few people trek into the Cabeza Prieta Wilderness to see sights such as this granite window.

(LEFT) A reclusive ponderosa pine stands among granite boulders, serving as a metaphor for the power of solitude. The scene lies in the Paiute Wilderness on the Arizona Strip of northwestern Arizona.

(FAR LEFT) A craggy, forbidding summit in the Paiute Wilderness affirms the persistence of life.

(PAGES 140 and 141) When economic hardships began to weaken the profitability of ranching in east-central Arizona's Aravaipa Canyon area in the 1970s, the beautiful canyon appeared destined for development. But ranchers Fred and Cliff Wood sold their 15,000 acres to The Nature Conservancy. The land was included in the Arizona Wilderness Act in 1984, preserving the saguaro forests and colorful sycamore and cottonwood trees lining the 11-mile creek. Some 200 species of birds reside in the canyon.

(RIGHT) Haunting orange and lilac light bathe the sandstone desert of the Paria Canyon-Vermilion Cliffs Wilderness.

(FAR RIGHT) In the same area, a sandstone basin saves rain water for creatures living in the wilderness.

(FOLLOWING PAGE) Baboquivari Peak is not a wilderness in the eyes of the U.S. government, but it is a sacred place for the Tohono O'odham people of Southern Arizona. In the words of the O'odham creation story: "And from his home among the tower cliffs and crags of Baboquivari, the lonely, cloud-veiled mountain peak, their Elder Brother, l'itoi, spirit of goodness, who must dwell in the center of all things, watches over them."